# SUBWAY

## THE STORY OF TUNNELS, TUBES, AND TRACKS

BY LARRY DANE BRIMNER
ILLUSTRATED BY NEIL WALDMAN

BOYDS MILLS PRESS

# Acknowledgments

My thanks to Faye Haun of the Museum of the City of New York, Marybeth Kavanagh, of the New York Historical Society, and Miriam Tierney of the New York Transit Museum, for their gracious assistance. A number of the illustrations in the book are based on materials found in the collections of these institutions.

— N. W.

New York Historical Society
Pages 3, 6, 7, 10, 20, 21 (bottom), 22

New York Transit Museum
Page 23

Library of Congress
Page 26

Museum of the City of New York
Page 5: Mayor McClellan on the First Formal Subway Inspection, 1904
Print Archives, Photo: Edwin Levick

Page 25: Groundbreaking at Bleecker & Greene Streets
On verso in pencil: "First Actual Work at Bleecker & Greene Sts." 1900
Print Archives, Gift of Mrs. William Barclay Parsons

Page 9: Orchard Street, Looking South from Hester Street, 1898
The Byron Collection

Jacket: The Broadway Pneumatic Underground Railway, View of Car in Motion
Print Archives, Gift of Ralph Moran

Text copyright © 2004 by Larry Dane Brimner, Trustee of the Brimner-Gregg Trust
Illustrations copyright © 2004 by Neil Waldman
All rights reserved

Published by Boyds Mills Press, Inc.
A Highlights Company
815 Church Street
Honesdale, Pennsylvania 18431
Printed in China
Visit our Web site at: www.boydsmillspress.com

First edition, 2004
The text of this book is set in 16-point Baskerville Oldface.
The illustrations are done with watercolor, acrylic, and pen & ink, on Arches hot-pressed watercolor paper.

10 9 8 7 6 5 4 3 2 1

Library of Congress Cataloging-in-Publication Data

Brimner, Larry Dane.
    Subway : the story of tunnels, tubes, and tracks /
by Larry Dane Brimner ;   illustrated by Neil Waldman.
    p.   cm.
    ISBN 1-59078-176-7 (alk. paper)
    1.   Subways—Juvenile literature.   I. Waldman, Neil.
II. Title.
TF845.B685 2004
388.4'28—dc22

2003026417

# OPENING DAY: THE NEW YORK SUBWAY

**C**HURCH BELLS AND FACTORY WHISTLES BEGAN chiming and blaring at exactly 2:00 that Thursday afternoon. It was October 27, 1904, and all of New York City was celebrating the opening of its subway, the seventh in the world. Unfortunately, the politicians and dignitaries who had gathered in City Hall to honor the occasion were not as punctual. Each speaker tried to outdo the

*George B. McClellan (center), mayor of New York, took a wild ride on the city's first subway train.*

preceding one, so that by the time the congratulatory speeches were over, the inaugural train's departure had been delayed by more than half an hour. But finally Mayor George B. McClellan led the select group of civic leaders to the subway kiosk in front of City Hall and down its stairs to the curved platform and waiting train. With a silver controller key, the mayor switched on the motor of New York's first official subway train.

The mayor was supposed to surrender control of the four-car train to a motorman. But he had never driven a subway train before, and the notion was tempting. Ignoring the pained expressions of many of his fellow dignitaries, he pressed the controller key and set the train in motion. It lurched out of the City Hall station with sudden starts and stops, while Frank M. Hedley, general manager of the subway, stood at the ready—one hand glued to the emergency brake and the other to the whistle to alert track workers to the danger.

Before long, the mayor's confidence swelled. The train shot northward through the tunnel at faster and faster speeds. Mr. Hedley, fearing an accident that would turn the public against the subway, urged the mayor to turn the controls over to the motorman. "No sir!" Mayor McClellan is reported to have said. "I'm running this train!"

Suddenly, the mayor's hand slipped off the throttle and hit the emergency brake. Steel scraped against steel. Sparks flew. The train came to a sudden stop that sent the top-hatted dignitaries sailing through the air.

Such was the excitement that filled New York City on opening day of the subway.

# A CITY ON THE MOVE

**E**VER SINCE MAYOR MCCLELLAN PUSHED the silver controller that started the first subway train, people have been traveling beneath the streets of New York City in a maze of tunnels, some as deep as 180 feet. Almost four million people a day scurry into them carrying packages, groceries, and other items

*On January 1, 1904, New York City dignitaries, riding in a canvas-covered car, took a tour of the subway, still under construction.*

from the world of daylight—or not carrying anything at all—and then are whisked away aboard the city's subway cars—some six thousand of them.

Today, many take the subway for granted. There was a time, however, when subways—underground railways—were unheard of. This might still be the case had it not been for the crush of humanity trying to eke out a living in cities on both sides of the Atlantic.

*Streetcars drawn by horses were among the many vehicles that jammed the streets of New York.*

# HORSE POWER

Cities were on the go in the early 1800s. The Industrial Revolution had made them booming centers of commerce, and people flocked into them to work and live. But at

*Traffic was tremendous on Broadway, with omnibuses passing City Hall approximately every fifteen seconds.*

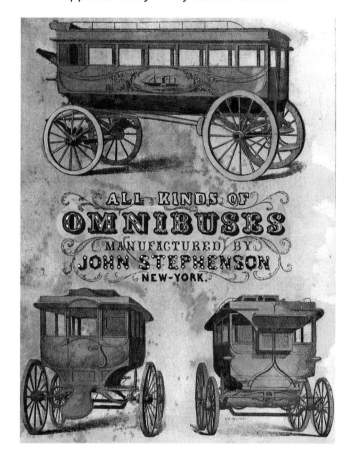

A SHOP +
A CARRIAGE LINE = BUS

*Have you ever thought about the word "bus"? In early nineteenth-century France, a gentleman named Baudry started a carriage line across from a shop run by another gentleman whose name was Omnes. Omnes's advertising slogan was "Omnes Omnibus," which, loosely translated, means "Omnes has something for everybody." It wasn't long before people began to associate the word* omnibus *with Baudry's carriage line, and eventually it came to mean a stage line that operates on a scheduled route. Over time, it was shortened to "bus."*

the same time that these very cities were exploding with growth, they were also at a complete standstill! Horse-drawn stagecoaches (called "omnibuses"), carriages, wagons, and newer horse-drawn streetcars on rails battled with one another to travel crowded urban streets.

Traffic was a mess! Drivers whipped their horses and yelled coarse words at each other as they bullied their way through streets that were almost impassable. Fistfights sometimes broke out when drivers couldn't advance their vehicles, further adding to the congestion. Pedestrians? People on foot barely stood a chance. The *New York Tribune* complained that you could travel halfway to Philadelphia "in less time than the length of Broadway."

If traffic was bad, the smell wasn't any better. With thousands of horses pulling vehicles of every description, streets and stables were full of manure. Owners of coach lines tried to convince the public that the smell was healthy because it brought "roses to the cheeks . . . and life to the intellect."

No one believed that. It stunk!

# FIRST, THE DREAM

**C**ITIES BEGAN TO BOOM WITH THE INTRODUCTION of steam engines powerful enough to drive machinery in the mid-1700s and, not too many years later, steam-driven locomotives in the first half of the nineteenth century. No longer bound to the land to scratch out a living, people could now find jobs in factories and mills, many of which were located in or near major cities. However, pay was usually poor. The workers couldn't afford to live any great distance from their jobs. So they put up makeshift housing that eventually became tenements, or slums. And as more people arrived, more factories and mills sprang up, and new calls for even

*FROM MUSCLES TO STEAM*

*It has been said that the single most important invention of the Industrial Revolution was the steam engine. It meant that people didn't have to rely on muscles to get things done. Who was behind it?*

*Many people credit James Watt (1736–1819) with the invention. The story goes that he got the idea after watching steam raise a kettle lid, but that's a myth. Watt simply made improvements to a steam engine designed by Thomas Newcomen (1663–1729). But even Newcomen's engine wasn't the first. As early as 1698, Thomas Savery (about 1650–1716) held a patent for a "Fire Engine" — a steam engine for "raising water" from mines. Although crude, it was one of the first steam-powered pumps. Savery improved upon an idea designed by Denis Papin (1647–about 1712), who used a rough version of a steam engine to supply water to the fountains of a palace garden.*

*So who invented the steam engine? Many people had a hand in it, as you can see, but it is Thomas Newcomen who is usually credited with the invention because his 1712 design was practical and widely used.*

more workers were put out. Before long, ten families were living in the same space that two families had occupied. In New York's Lower East Side, where many new immigrants sought housing, twenty people might share one small room. Simply, cities were overcrowded. Add to this mix an abundance of horse-drawn vehicles, and you can see why the *New York Herald* declared, "Something more is needed. . . ."

*Manhattan's Lower East Side: congested streets and overcrowded tenements.*

*Long lines of trolleys and trains rumbled over the Brooklyn Bridge.*

Dreamers on both sides of the Atlantic had lots of ideas for fixing the cities of the 1800s—from underground horseways to moving sidewalks. What they shared was the notion of rapid transit—transportation that runs without any interference from other traffic. Unfortunately, their ideas were all impractical.

It was London that first took action. Each day thousands of people arrived by ferry across the Thames River. Thousands more

*Marc Isambard Brunel planned to tunnel under the Thames.*

crossed London Bridge on foot. Movement across London Bridge was so slow that products sometimes wilted or spoiled before merchants could sell them. There had to be another way of getting people and products to and from the city, and Marc Isambard Brunel had a plan.

Brunel had watched a shipworm with keen interest one day as it ate its way through some wood, the sharp shells on either side of its head giving protection at its forward end while it lined the passage from behind with a secretion that turned hard. Although tunnels were common in the 1800s, building them was always fraught with the danger of collapse. Brunel's plan was to build a mechanical shipworm to tunnel under the Thames and provide another path into London. He tinkered with designs until he came up with something he called a *shield*.

Brunel's shield held thirty-four compartments, each with a removable oak plank. Miners inside the compartments would remove the planks, dig out four and a half inches of earth, replace the planks, and move the shield forward. Then they would repeat the process. At the rear of the shield, a team of workers and bricklayers removed dirt and lined the tunnel. For the 1800s, this was a

*THE GREAT BORE*

*When Marc Isambard Brunel started digging,* The Times of London *called the Thames Tunnel a "great national enterprise." Their enthusiasm faded, though, after years of snail-paced progress. Before the tunnel was completed, the* Times *had dubbed Brunel's tunnel "the Great Bore."*

*Tunneling under London using an improved metal version of Brunel's wooden shield.*

marvel of engineering. It protected workers as they tunneled through the earth, but it wasn't perfect.

Work began on the Thames Tunnel in 1825, and before it was completed and officially opened eighteen years later, it had claimed numerous lives in mishap after mishap. Even so, the shield proved that tunnels need not be limited by boundaries of water, and it cleared the way for subways of the future.

# SMOKE UNDER LONDON

**T**HE WORLD'S FIRST TRUE SUBWAY HAD ITS beginning in 1843 in London, when Sir Charles Pearson, who is sometimes called the "Father of the Subway," began talking about an underground railway. Pearson argued that an underground railway would eliminate street traffic and relocate the poor to the countryside, thus solving London's two biggest problems.

Many people didn't like the idea of an underground railway. The underground drummed up images of demons and devils, not to mention graveyards!

But Pearson was a patient man. It's a good thing.  His idea didn't catch on until fifteen years later, and then not until after he had outlined a financial plan that would make it possible. Even so, digging on the London Underground didn't start until 1860.

The main cause of delay was ventilation. The air in existing tunnels was foul. Smoke that belched from steam locomotives would make travel underground unbearable. Sir John Fowler, engineer for the Metropolitan Railway, had a solution: a smokeless engine. But "Fowler's Ghost," as his engine came to be called, made only one run. It was a flop.

Another engine was designed. This one stored the smoke in chambers behind the engine when it was in a tunnel and released the smoke when the engine reached a ventilation shaft or came out of the tunnel. It wasn't perfect, but it was enough for the real work of digging to finally begin.

Since there were fears that digging under buildings might topple them, engineers decided to place the tracks in shallow trenches under the streets. These would not threaten the foundations of buildings and would also be easier to ventilate. Once the tracks were in place, bricklayers built sidewalls and a roof. Then workers covered the whole thing over and replaced the road. This "cut-and-cover" method of tunneling caused nearly as many problems as the subway was expected to solve because, for three years, many of London's main roadways were torn up and people had to crowd other routes to travel.

Progress was slow. Disgruntled property owners filed lawsuit after lawsuit. Then at one point the Fleet Ditch broke into the

Constructing the London subway caused chaos, as trenches tore up existing streets.

trench. The Fleet Ditch was a river that had been covered over—as had been many of London's rivers—and now was used as a sewer. When the flooding was over, ten feet of sewage filled the track bed.

Nonetheless, the Metropolitan Line eventually opened. On January 9, 1863, London became the first city in the world to have a subway. When the train opened to the general public, thirty thousand people went for the ride. It was so popular with Londoners that they wanted this fast (about twenty miles per hour) new way of travel extended. The London Underground has been expanding ever since.

# ELECTRIFIED!

**T**HE ELECTRIC INDUSTRY WAS STILL IN INFANCY in the 1800s, but inventors were busy tinkering. In Germany, Werner von Siemens figured out a way to use electricity as a source of energy in 1866. It was probably his most important contribution to the electrical field because it paved the way to electric-powered engines.

In fact, a few years later at the Berlin Industrial Exhibition of 1879, Siemens gave demonstration rides to the public in a small electric-powered locomotive. It zipped along at an amazing eight miles per hour!

The next year, Thomas Edison unveiled his own electric-powered locomotive. It reached forty miles per hour—a speed that terrified Edison's passengers! But Edison wasn't really interested in transportation. It was an Edison associate, Frank Julian Sprague, who thought that electricity was the future of railways.

Sprague joined Edison's team of researchers in 1883. The next year he set up his own company, the Sprague Electric Railway and Motor Company. There, he created a much-improved electric motor and went about trying to convince operators of elevated railway lines—those that ran on tracks above the streets—that electric power was the way to go. They were content with their spark-spewing steam locomotives. So Sprague turned to streetcars.

*Thomas Edison*

His first project was to electrify a small streetcar line in Saint Joseph, Missouri. It was a success and paved the way for him to design an entire streetcar system in Richmond, Virginia. Another success. Soon, Sprague-designed streetcars could be seen in cities throughout North America and the world.

*Frank Julian Sprague*

But Sprague didn't rest. He came up with something he called a "multiple-unit control" system. Electric motors weren't powerful enough to pull many cars. Sprague's new system meant that each car could be outfitted with a motor of its own that could be controlled by a driver in the lead car. Suddenly, trains could be as long as necessary. The days of soot- and smoke-filled subway tunnels were numbered.

# NEW YORK! NEW YORK!

**TRACKS AND MORE TRACK**

*With the success of the London Underground, other cities wanted subways, too. Glasgow, Scotland, opened its subway in 1886 with cars that were pulled by cable. In Hungary, Budapest became the first city on the continent of Europe to have an electric subway. It opened in 1896. Boston got a jump on its rival, New York, when in 1897 it launched a line of electric-powered underground streetcars—North America's first official subway.*

*On July 19, 1900, just twenty months after digging had begun, Paris, France, opened its Metro. Then in 1902, it was Berlin's turn. Subways had caught on.*

**W**HILE OTHER CITIES WERE BUILDING SUBWAYS, all New York's leaders had managed to do was talk about one. Indeed, when Mayor Robert A. Van Wyck finally hoisted a silver spade to break ground for New York's subway system on March 24, 1900, the city had been talking about one for more than thirty years.

What had caused the delay? Politics and greed. William "Boss" Tweed, a corrupt politician who ruled New York City, blocked every attempt to approve the building of a subway. Why wouldn't he? Tweed received part of every omnibus fare collected, and the deal was making him a very rich man. A subway would cut into his profits.

*William "Boss" Tweed tried to stop the New York subway.*

*Alfred Ely Beach, the man who built a secret subway*

Alfred Ely Beach believed that subways were the solution to New York's snarled traffic and crowded living conditions. But he knew that "Boss" Tweed wouldn't allow anything to compete with the omnibus operators. So Beach did the only thing that made sense: he built a subway in secret, tunneling at night from the basement of a clothing store on Broadway.

*Inside Beach's pneumatic railway car*

His plan was to use wind to push a railway car through an underground tunnel. It wasn't an original idea. In England, the post office had installed an air-powered, or pneumatic, railway in 1863 to move mail more quickly under London. (You may have seen a pneumatic tube in action at the drive-up window of a bank. The post office's pneumatic railway worked the same way, except that the carriers were large enough to hold packages—and even people!)

When Beach opened his subway to the public on February 28, 1870, a grandfather clock, fountain, and grand piano welcomed them to the platform. His "Pneumatic Transit" was an instant success. Its one car, a fancy affair, held twenty-two passengers and was blown through the block-long tunnel (312 feet) at about six miles per hour by wind from a giant fan. When it reached the end, the fan was reversed and the car moved in the opposite direction. During its first year of operation, more than four hundred thousand passengers paid a quarter each to make the trip.

*Passengers line up for Alfred Ely Beach's pneumatic railway.*

In spite of the subway's success, Tweed was powerful enough to twice block plans for its expansion. It wasn't until 1873 that Beach finally got legislative approval to go ahead with his subway. By then, though, he had run out of money. He ended up renting out the tunnel, first as a shooting gallery and then as a wine cellar, before he closed it for good.

*Though popular with the public, Beach's pneumatic railway was opposed by "Boss" Tweed, who stopped it dead in its tracks.*

# ENTER
# AUGUST BELMONT JR.

**T**HE CITY THAT HAD INTRODUCED THE ELEVATED railway to the world in 1868 was now taking a backseat to those cities with rapid subway systems. Then an interesting thing happened: Tweed was investigated for corruption in 1871 and sent to jail. Suddenly, he was out of the way.

Even so, politicians continued to bicker about the need for a subway, even as tenements grew more crowded and traffic barely moved. Then came the blizzard of 1888. Called "the Great White Hurricane," the blizzard struck on March 11 and dumped 21 inches of snow on the city. Wind gusts blew it into great, mounding drifts. People were stranded in their offices, and elevated trains and horse-drawn carriages were stuck. It was impossible to deliver groceries and goods. The city was paralyzed, and politicians finally realized that something had to be done about its transportation.

Now, only one obstacle remained: paying for the project. Building a subway was a tremendous undertaking, and the city, by law, was required to limit its debt. Abram S. Hewitt, a former mayor of New York City, proposed a solution: the city would maintain ownership of the subway, but private companies would build and operate it. The Rapid Transit Commission was formed to

*THE ELEVATED RAILWAYS*

*The world's first elevated railway line and New York's nod to rapid transit opened in 1868. Charles T. Harvey's West Side & Yonkers Patent Railway was pulled by a continuously moving loop of steal cable.*

*Unfortunately, the cable was prone to breaking, and so Harvey's company failed.*

*Elevated railways, however, lived on, with steam-powered locomotives replacing cable power. But steam-powered locomotives had problems, too. They rained down smoke, soot, and cinders on people below! They frightened teams of horses! Thus, the heyday of elevated railways mostly came to an end, the most notable exception being the Chicago "L," which in 1895 became the first electric-powered elevated railway in the United States and continues to be a popular transportation choice among Chicagoans.*

oversee the details, and in 1894 it chose William Barclay Parsons as chief engineer. John B. McDonald, a contractor, won the bid for the actual construction. But when McDonald had difficulty raising the money necessary to begin work, he turned to August Belmont Jr.

*August Belmont Jr. financed the construction of the subway.*

August Belmont Jr. was a money man. He saw the subway as a good investment and was happy to take over McDonald's contract. He formed two companies: a construction company, for which he provided six million dollars, and the Interborough Rapid Transit Company (IRT), which would tend to the subway's day-to-day

operation. Then he hired McDonald as the contractor, and building began.

Chief engineer Parsons thought it would be best to use the cut-and-cover method of excavation to build shallow trenches within fifteen to twenty feet of the surface. Then he had a stroke of inspiration: he proposed laying four tracks, two for trains serving local commuters over short distances and two for "express" trains, which would make fewer stops and help speed passengers to their destinations. At the time, it was an idea that would set the New York subway apart from any other subway in the world.

*Dreaming the future: Engineers in the late 1860s imagined what the New York Subway might look like.*

For two years, Parsons and his "sandhogs," the workers who excavated the tunnels, managed to avoid any serious mishaps. Then disaster struck. On January 27, 1902, Moses Epps slipped into a dynamite-storage shed for lunch and lighted a candle to warm his hands. The resulting blast left the area looking much like a war zone. Accounts vary, but at least five people were killed and more than one hundred eighty were injured. Amazingly, Epps received only bruises. Other mishaps followed, the worst perhaps being a delayed blast in October 1903 that caught a crew of returning workers by surprise. This time at least fifty men were killed, and scores of others injured.

But work continued. When, at last, the subterranean wonder opened on October 27, 1904, Mayor McClellan had the time of his life showing it off to the assembled dignitaries aboard the first official train. Of course, there was that tense moment after his hand slipped from the controller and brought the train to a screeching halt. But since no one was injured in the mishap, the mayor saw no reason to turn the controls over to the motorman. Why, he was just beginning to get a feel for the great machine! In short order, and likely to the alarm of the now disheveled dignitaries, he took the train's speed even higher—to an unheard-of forty-five miles per hour. It rocketed down the straightaways. It careened around curves until, at last, McClellan suddenly tired of his experience. He turned the train over to motorman George L. Morrison, who brought the train to the end of its run safely and on schedule.

*NEW YORK FOR A NICKEL*
*Unlike the subways in London or Paris, where fares were determined by the distance traveled, the New York subway had only one fare: a nickel each direction, no matter how far a person traveled. As the subway spread, developers bought up farmland along its route. They built new houses and apartments, and workers—abandoning the crowded Lower East Side for the wide, open spaces of Upper Manhattan, the Bronx, Brooklyn, and Queens—began to fill them. Commutes that would have been unthinkable before the subway now took only minutes and, thanks to the nickel fare, were affordable.*

*Within ten years of opening, the subway was serving nearly one billion riders a year. The nickel fare was critical to the subway's success and to the simultaneous expansion of both the subway and New York City. The fare remained a nickel for nearly fifty years when, in 1948, it finally was raised to a dime.*

*Building tunnels under Broadway in New York*

Later, the subway opened to the public, and the response was overwhelming. More than one hundred fifty thousand people paid the nickel fare to "do" the subway. One newspaper declared that New York had become "the city of human prairie dogs." As you might imagine, the crowd was at times unruly, but in spite of this, the subway captured the hearts and imaginations of the public. Suddenly, there were songs ("The Subway Express") and new dances (the "Subway Express Two-Step"). And the subway grew. As it did, it helped build New York City upward—because the subway brought in more workers to fill the skyscrapers—and outward—as farmland gave way to development along the tracks.

*In 1964, New York's Times Square station was a busy place, with millions of people taking the subway to the World's Fair in Flushing. Today, an estimated fifty-three million people a year pass through the Times Square station.*

# BACK TO THE FUTURE

**I**N THE BEGINNING, SUBWAYS WERE SEEN AS solutions to all the problems of city life. But as more and more people moved into them, cities remained crowded. Traffic continued to be congested.

Then came the automobile. With its introduction and the development of high-speed expressways, subways—for a while—became dinosaurs. No one wanted to build new systems, and many of those cities that already possessed them allowed their subways to decline.

But just as cities in the nineteenth century had experienced crowding and crippling traffic, modern cities soon began to experience their own problems with congestion. Over time, many expressways came to a standstill. Once again people complained about gridlock and lengthy travel times. It wasn't long until modern city planners began to look backward to see their futures. What they saw were subways.

Since the mid-twentieth century, subways have been booming. Cities such as London, Moscow, and Tokyo have all seen their subway systems expand—Tokyo's subways with large, underground shopping malls resembling underground cities. Others, such as Toronto; Mexico City; Washington, D.C.; San Francisco; and Los Angeles, have invested in brand-new systems.

*THE CHUNNEL*
*Advances in tunnel-boring machinery have come a long way since Brunel's shield. Since the late 1800s, the English have wanted a tunnel under the channel that separates England and France. Nobody knew how to do it. Then in the 1980s, the idea resurfaced, and this time engineers had the know-how.*

*Work began in 1987, with digging from both the English and French sides of the channel. In 1990, the two tunnels met in the middle, some one hundred fifty feet under the bottom of the sea. The 31-mile-long (23 are underwater) Chunnel, or "Eurotunnel," as it is officially called, opened in May 1994. Actually three tunnels in one, the Chunnel provides a 20-minute train passage for people, who remain with their vehicles, and freight. Imagine this: rubble from the tunnel added 90 acres—about 68 football fields—to England's size!*

**DID YOU KNOW?**

*The New York subway is the longest in the world, having more than 700 miles of track. That's almost enough to stretch from New York City to Chicago. Not all of the track runs underground, however. Depending on a line's history, the neighborhood it passes through, the height of the subsurface water, and the lay of the land, parts of the subway run along the surface to keep the incline of the track manageable.*

Today, subways are not seen as the sole solution to the problems of everyday city life. Instead, they are seen for what they are—marvelous people movers that do their job quickly, efficiently, and affordably. When part of a larger system of people movers—one that includes buses and surface and overhead rails—subways can help reduce urban crowding, traffic gridlock, and our impact on the environment. But they are more. They are monuments to the people who first dreamed of them, and to the people who ride them.

# Author's Note

I've always been fascinated by subways. As a teenager growing up in rural California with parents pressing me to get a driver's license, I put them off by predicting that someday I would live in a city with a subway, and so wouldn't require a knowledge of driving. Although that prophecy never came true, I have traveled to many of the great cities of the world that have subway systems. My fascination has turned into appreciation—for at their best, subways are exciting, swift, efficient, economical, and ecologically sound.

Many different sources were used as references for this book, and I am grateful to the many researchers and writers who helped unfold the subway story before me. I am most appreciative of Benson Bobrick for his groundbreaking book *Labyrinths of Iron: A History of the World's Subways*, and to Clifton Hood for *722 Miles: The Building of the Subways and How They Transformed New York*. Several other titles were indispensable: *London Under London: A Subterranean Guide* by Richard Trench and Ellis Hillman; *Cash, Tokens, and Transfers: A History of Urban Mass Transit in North America* by Brian J. Cudahy; *Underneath New York* by Harry Granick; *Tunneling to the Future: The Story of the Great Subway Expansion That Saved New York* by Peter Derrick; *Subways of the World* by Stan Fischler; *The Book of New York Firsts: Unusual, Arcane, and Fascinating Facts in the Life of New York City* by Henry Moscow; and finally, *The Jubilee Line Extension* by Kenneth Powell. Material and brief quotations from these references have allowed me to put a human touch on urban conditions in the presubway world.

Special thanks are due Victoria Amadin of London Underground Limited; Caroline Warhurst, Library and Information Services Manager of the London Transport Museum; Jaye Furlonger, Assistant Archivist of the New York Transit Museum; and Paul Matus for their quick responses to my queries.

Larry Dane Brimner
Tucson, Arizona

# Index

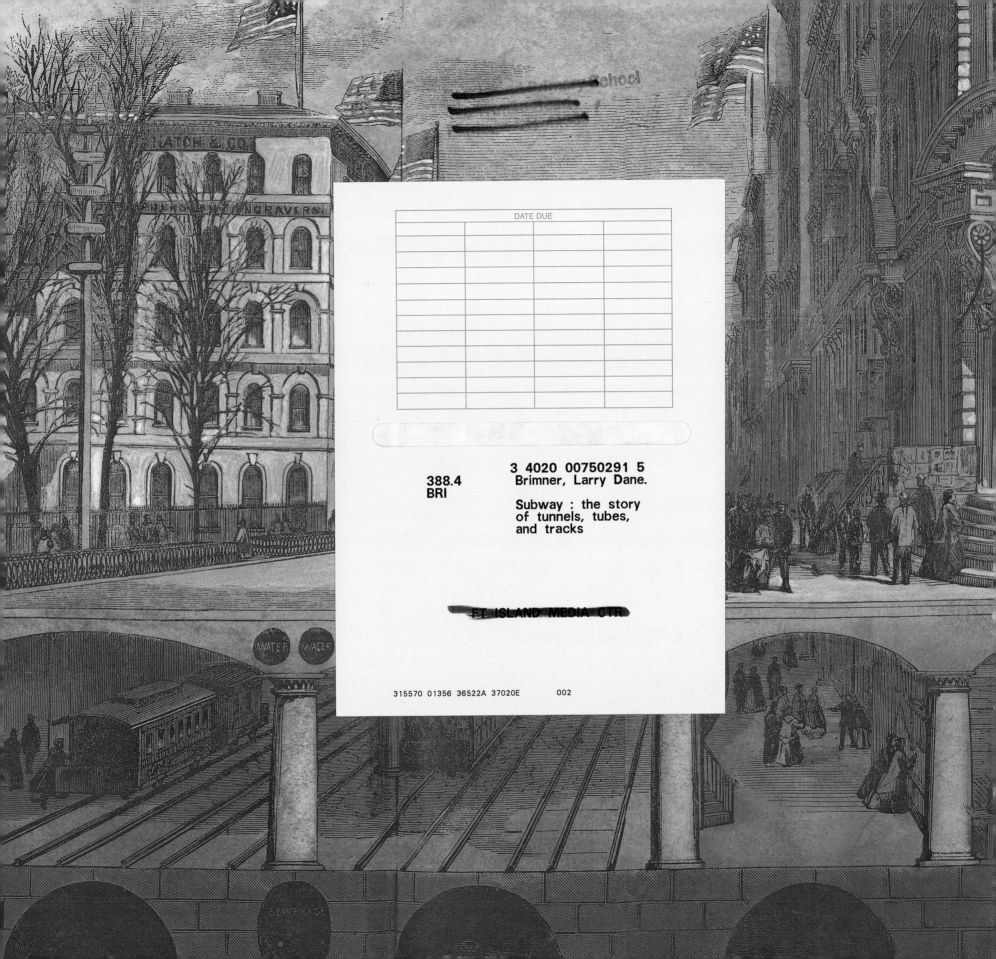